Through the Roof

Mark 2:1–12

(Jesus Heals a Paralyzed Man)

Mary Manz Simon

Illustrated by Dennis Jones

CPH™

ST. LOUIS

For David Kopp
Proverbs 3:5–6

Books by Mary Manz Simon

Hear Me Read Level 1
What Next? CPH
Drip Drop, CPH
Jibber Jabber, CPH
Hide the Baby, CPH
Toot! Toot! CPH
Bing! CPH
Whoops! CPH
Send a Baby, CPH
A Silent Night, CPH
Follow That Star, CPH
Row the Boat, CPH
Rumble, Rumble, CPH
Who Will Help? CPH
Sit Down, CPH
Come to Jesus, CPH
Too Tall, Too Small, CPH
Hurry, Hurry! CPH
Where Is Jesus? CPH

Hear Me Read Level 2
The No-Go King, CPH
Hurray for the Lord's Army! CPH
The Hide-and-Seek Prince, CPH
Daniel and the Tattletales, CPH
The First Christmas, CPH
Through the Roof, CPH
A Walk on the Waves, CPH
Thank You, Jesus, CPH

God's Children Pray, CPH
My First Diary, CPH
52 Ways to Raise Happy, Loving Kids
  Thomas Nelson Publishing

Little Visits on the Go, CPH
Little Visits 1-2-3, CPH
Little Visits with Jesus, CPH
More Little Visits with Jesus, CPH

Copyright © 1994 Concordia Publishing House
3558 S. Jefferson Avenue, St. Louis, MO 63118-3968
Manufactured in the United States of America

Library of Congress Cataloging in Publication Data

Simon, Mary Manz, 1948–
   Through the roof / Mary Manz Simon; illustrated by Dennis Jones.
      p.   cm.   — (Hear me read. Level 2)
   1. Healing of the man sick of the palsy (Miracle)—Juvenile literature. 2. Bible stories—N.T. Gospels. [1. Healing of the man sick of the palsy (Miracle) 2. Jesus Christ—Miracles. 3. Bible stories—N.T.) I. Jones, Dennis ill. II. Title. III. Series: Simon, Mary Manz, 1948– Hear me read. Level 2.
BT367.H45S55   1994
226.7'09505—dc20   93-36193

   2 3 4 5 6 7 8 9 10   03 02 01 00 99 98 97 96 95

"Have you heard?" asked a man.
"Jesus is back.
Jesus is back in town."

"How do you know?" asked his friend.

"Everybody is talking about it,"
said the man.
"Jesus is back.
He is preaching about God's love
right now."

"Jesus?" asked a sick man.
"Jesus is back?"

"Yes," said his friends.
"He is preaching at a house
right now."

"Please," begged the sick man.
"Take me to Jesus.
Jesus has healed others.
Jesus can heal me."

The men looked at each other.
They looked at their sick friend.

"Jesus *has* healed others," said
one man.

"Please," begged the sick man.
"Take me to Jesus.
Jesus has healed others.
Jesus can heal me."

The men looked at each other.
They looked at their sick friend.

"We could go slowly," said one man.

They picked up the bed.
One step, another step.
The bed swayed back and forth.
They walked very slowly.

"We will help," called some
more friends.
"Where are you going?"

"We are going to see Jesus," said
the sick man.
"Jesus has healed others.
Jesus can heal me."

Slowly, slowly they moved.
One step, another step.
The bed swayed back and forth,
back and forth.

They saw a crowd of people.

"Jesus is preaching," said the man.
"Jesus is preaching in that house."

The friends could not hear Jesus.
They could not see Jesus.
They could only see the crowd
of people.

"Come up," whispered one friend.
"You can hear Jesus."

"Yes, yes. I can hear Jesus," said one friend.
"I can hear Jesus preach."

"Look," said another friend.
"Now I can see Jesus.
I can see and hear Jesus."

"Please," called the sick man.
"Please take me to Jesus."

The men looked at each other.
They looked at their sick friend.

"We could go slowly," said one man.

Slowly, slowly they moved.
One step, another step.
The bed swayed back and forth, back
and forth.

"You can hear Jesus," said one man.
"Now you can hear Jesus."

"Please," begged the sick man.
"Please take me to Jesus.
Jesus has healed others.
Jesus can heal me."

The men looked at each other.
They looked at their sick friend.

"Jesus has healed others," said
one man.
"We could go very slowly."

Slowly, slowly they moved.
The bed swayed back and forth, back
and forth.

Jesus looked up.
The people looked up.
Jesus looked at the men.

Jesus said to the sick man,
"Your sins are forgiven."

"Oh!" said the people.
The people looked at Jesus.
The people looked at each other.

Jesus looked at the sick man.

"Now," said Jesus.
"Pick up your bed now.
Pick up your bed and go home."

Everyone watched.
The man stood up.
He picked up his bed.

"See what Jesus did?" the man said.
"Jesus healed me."

The man took his bed and walked
home.

The people said,
"Look what Jesus did!"

About the Author
Mary Manz Simon holds a doctoral degree in education with a specialty in early childhood education. She has taught at levels from preschool through postgraduate. Dr. Simon has also authored *God's Children Pray,* the best-selling *Little Visits with Jesus, More Little Visits with Jesus, Little Visits 1-2-3, Little Visits on the Go, My First Diary,* and the Hear Me Read Level 1 Bible stories series. She and her husband, the Reverend Henry A. Simon, are the parents of three children.